Utterly

PS Cottier

Utterly

Acknowledgements

Poems in this collection have appeared in the following publications, sometimes in a slightly different form:

Australian Poetry Journal, Australian Catholic University Prize for Poetry chapbooks (various years), *Axon: Creative Explorations, Best Australian Science Writing* anthology, *The Canberra Times, Cordite, Embody* anthology, *Eureka Street, Grieve* anthology, *Images, The Mozzie*, New England Writers Centre website, *Mnemosyne, New Shoots* anthology, *Not Very Quiet, Plumwood Mountain*, Project 366, *Right Now, Wild* anthology, *Verity La*.

Some poems were first published on the poet's blog, pscottier.com. 'The ineffable boredom of Polonius', published on the blog, was included in *Under Sedation*, a theatre work created and directed by Adele Chynoweth performed at the Street Theatre, Canberra, 2017.

The title *Utterly* refers to the phrase 'changed utterly' from W.B. Yeats's 'Easter 1916', but has no reference to Ireland, or to beauty, terrible or otherwise.

Utterly
ISBN 978 1 76041 947 9
Copyright © PS Cottier 2020

First published 2020 by
GINNINDERRA PRESS
PO Box 3461 Port Adelaide 5015
www.ginninderrapress.com.au

Contents

Preface	7

1 Taking the temperature of time

Reading the frog economy	13
The dusky grasswren	14
Only the budgie	15
Professor Pangloss's guide to ornithology	16
On nothing	18
The Cootamundra Wattle	20
A nice trip with plastics	22
Climate change (no gears)	23
On the death of the V8	25
Not one cent	26
Fordite	27
Spectre	28
Going to the coast	29
'The crowd was famish'd by degrees...'	30
Lacertilian	31
Feral	33
Cane toad speaks	34
Cane toad continues	36
Mining time	37
The canary, the pony, and the man	38
Fry up	39
Mo(n)de	40
My indifference is supreme, says Pluto	41

2 Furthernear

On the couch	45
Night camels	46
Four times a week	47

My body's architecture	48
She who they shall call uncool	50
Not sorting it out	51
Grief before grief	52
Seat 13B	53
Intersections	54
Locus	55
How to make depression worse…	56
Thoughts like lollies in the cinema	57
On average	59
Interrobang	60
Stepping over, stepping around	62
Burning the donkey	63
Three aspects of Australian racism	65
Seven ways to look at a sculpture	66
Three ways to look at crochet	67
The ineffable boredom of Polonius	68
A brief history of fun	71
'For services to charity…'	72
Heft and leaf	74
The hole	76
Who is this woman?	77
A hard poem to market	79
100 or more holes in my bucket	81

Preface

Utterly, the title of this volume, references W.B. Yeats's 'Easter 1916', written in the aftermath of a failed Irish uprising against the English. The line 'all changed, changed utterly', described Ireland after the British execution of its revolutionary leaders. Cottier, like Yeats, also writes about irreversible change – but in this case, the setting is contemporary Australia and anthropogenic climate change. This book begins at a distance, taking stock of almost unfathomable environmental damage, before telescoping into the inner, personal world of the poet.

Cottier pulls no punches on the topic of human-induced climate change, beginning her elegy for the Murray cod, 'Fry up', with a series of epigraphs from *State of the Climate 2018*:

> Australia's climate has warmed by just over 1°C since 1910, leading to an increase in the frequency of extreme heat events... There has been a decline of around 11 per cent in April–October rainfall in the south-east of Australia since the late 1990s... Streamflow has decreased across southern Australia... Oceans around Australia have warmed by around 1°C since 1910...

We are reminded, very early in this collection, that we're all in deep trouble.

Like 'Fry up', many of Cottier's poems bear witness to vanishing Australian wildlife – the birds and animals we grew up with (Gen X people like her and me, at any rate). 'If frogs were currency,' she writes, 'I grew up in a time of wealth' but in today's profit-driven age 'I'd invest in bottled, pure water if I were you. Read the labels: Guaranteed to contain no frog.'

Even more cutting is her 'Professor Pangloss's guide to ornithology': 'That little finch, / the black-throated one, / well it just loves coal. / That's how it got the black throat', and later, 'Adani will be just the thing / to help the little birds adapt.'

There is no denying that the Australia of the poet's youth, with its pristine beaches, its bushlands with koalas and skinks, has 'all changed, changed utterly'. In Queensland, the Great Barrier Reef is bleaching under Adani's coal-laden waters. 'Two thousand kilometres / grinning white forever', she writes, 'and rumours of fish'. Our marine birds and animals are tangled and choked in plastic. 'Plastics is the love that will never die', she says. 'Never shall it decompose.'

No doubt is left as to who bears responsibility for this annihilation of species. One of the crowning jewels of this collection, 'The crowd was famish'd by degrees...' (after Byron's 'Darkness', 1816) states,

> And now we sit in the smeltered world,
> and see the crowds famish'd by degrees;
> the crops of dust, the skies weeping
> or obstinately dry. Look on our works,
> the world must say, as some drown in
> lakes of manmade excess. Ah George,
> would that it were one volcano, one brief
> year without a summer, as we ask
> what dread creature, and know it to be us.

Like all compelling poets, PS Cottier takes what is most private, most personal – that which shames her, or makes her vulnerable – and rather than hiding those things, she publishes them. This is the superpower of poets. Because some things can only live in the dark – like those orchids growing under permanent cloud in the Andes – even a moment of direct sunlight will kill them. Poets, at least the good ones, are demon-killers – liberating themselves and, by extension, their readers through acts of courageous truth-telling.

In a book condemning the fossil fuel industry, Cottier writes of her passion for V8 cars – 'I am no metalhead Miss Havisham, / clutching a chamois, all wept out. / And yet, when I die, I hope the chariot, / swinging down, is a lowered, purple V8.' It's okay, she's telling us – we are all human, flawed and beautiful as birds. By the middle of this book, one realises that *Utterly* is a portrait of a nation manifesting inside a woman.

Throughout this volume, Cottier unflinchingly examines ageing, grief and violence in the world and in herself. Her skin, she tells us, is no longer carrara glass, / smooth, unpocked and sleek, / throwing back what the looker would see. / I am become adobe, roughly applied.' Her gaze is merciless. 'She who they shall call uncool' describes a person unknown as 'a pomelo amongst oranges / sarsaparilla amongst the Coke, / iceberg lettuce next to Italian mix, / or a prawn cocktail. Limping entrée.' No special mercy is shown to poets, and especially not for herself. Cottier describes commuters stepping over a 'collapsed man the vinculum / dividing the rear leg from the front', concluding, 'And some of us step over and around / by using him for clever poems. / Grounding them in a certain reality – / restrained muggers of another's pain.' The strength of these poems rests on the fact that the poet never exempts herself from responsibility.

Reading these poems is an act of participating in another person's inner world. The poet has lost her father and can't bear to sort out his things 'if they stay in the bag, / my ex-toy, his service medals, / one part of me doesn't have to, / have to say he's dead.' And while this inner world is coloured by loss – of fathers, of reefs poisoned by Adani, birds lost to coal – it is the poet's self-deprecating humour that provides balance. The ineffable boredom of Polonius, for example: 'Hamlet had a go; stabbing him behind the arras, / which does not mean what you may think it means / if you didn't *do* Shakespeare in your degree.'

PS Cottier is not an easy poet – she does not play nicely with the other poets, is not domesticated. *Utterly* is the work of a significant Australian writer. It is also the work of a smoking, muscle-car loving, clever as fuck, Canberra girl – devastatingly truthful, terrifying and funny. I defy any poetry lover to read these poems and not fall a little in love with the author.

Judith Nangala Crispin

1

Taking the temperature of time

Reading the frog economy

So if frogs were currency, I grew up in a time of wealth. We'd pour dozens of lively taddies into buckets; little ones like commas in the rich brown pages of the ponds, betwixters sprouting legs like exclamation marks, and the fat copper adults. They weren't like rare coins back then when I was a lass, they were just as common as two-cent pieces; nursery rhyme familiars. Every suburban bog housed their evening pukpuks of attraction, their sudden bursts of swim.

Ah, but since then, since that once upon a time, it's been a real bear market for the frog economy. We've cleansed the ponds of amphibious poetry. Soft bodies, splayed feet are not a good bet on the futures exchange; I'd invest in bottled, pure water if I were you. Read the labels: Guaranteed to contain no frog (music or body or magical transformation or splash! or the foaming floating islands of egg).

In my memory I flick every rock and find a frog deposit. We'd withdraw them with no worry; take them home in triumphant ice cream containers, a whole Europe of minor princes carried by a court of pesky kids. Now a child blessed with luck might be shown a frog as if it were formed from a weak and discoloured gold; about to melt away, first legs, then body. See that, children? That's a frog. No kissing, please.

The dusky grasswren

Amytornis purnelli

They live in spinifex
sharp as needles.
Slips of twitchable feather
avoid piercing
by miraculous instinct.

Piping shrilly,
higher than some can hear,
they pop up.
The Scottish word wee
is all I can think of.

Cats relish them,
but the spinifex,
sharp as cats' claws,
gives them
almost a chance.

They lurk,
way below the parrots
who flaunt and flap.
Grant that such tiny brown
still finds islands of spike.

Only the budgie

Melopsittacus undulatus

We saw the birds – rufous and dusky,
spoon-billed and barking,
white-breasted, white-backed, and red-capped.

The largest with its three letter name.
The smallest, buzzing like a large bee.
The rarest of all (in the Northern Territory).

One quarter of all Australia's birds,
in two weeks. Not too shabby.
But one that I knew well was not there.

I felt like calling *budgie budgie budgie*,
or asking who's a pretty boy?
(After all, isn't that what one does?)

But the budgies were elsewhere,
annoyingly elsewhere, chasing water or seed.
Unseen, ten thousand sleek green bodies.

We saw the others – hooded and crested,
water-diving, bower-building, desert-dwelling,
city savvy or painfully shy.

Only the budgie asserted its right
to avoid us, to sneer at our lists.
Most-often caged. Inexorably wild.

Professor Pangloss's guide to ornithology

That little finch,
the black-throated one,
well, it just loves coal.
That's how it got the black throat,
through rubbing itself against small pieces
strewn around here and there,
over many many years.
With more coal, it will become all black,
just like those peppered moths,
who turned delightfully sooty
as trees and walls darkened
in industrious England.
That began to happen from 1819,
so a finch jubilee will be a nice way
to celebrate. Adani will be just the thing
to help the little birds adapt,
a concept that has really come into its own,
as I understand it, since my heyday.
What could be sweeter than a dusky finch,
blending into its new environment?
A regular little night parrot of the day,
and a challenge for the avid twitcher.
Everyone loves the blackbird,
with its beautiful song.

How much more the antics
of the coal-finch, cheeping
and fluttering through the belch,
or walking on the Basin of Galilee?
We really need to work that field.

Professor Pangloss was Candide's tutor. The last line of the poem is a flagrant misuse of the last line of Voltaire's *Candide, or Optimism*, spoken by Candide.
The finch: https://en.wikipedia.org/wiki/Black-throated_finch
The moths: https://www.bbc.com/news/science-environment-36424768
The coal: https://www.statedevelopment.qld.gov.au/assessments-and-approvals/carmichael-coal-mine-and-rail-project.html

On nothing

'Time doesn't mean anything when you're about to…have water lapping at your door.' – Peter Dutton, 2015

She's wading through water,
and wading through
our liking for the second car,
the nightly dose of super-cool air,
or of sweet winter heat.
Because we can't be bothered
to rise from the couch
like chilly plump angels
and put on one, just one,
of the many waiting clothes
tucked away in a fly-in wardrobe –
those fluffy ghosts hanging in time –
she's wading, wading,
until she must learn to swim.

A second woman can't farm
what she used to farm
because seasons have transmogrified.
Top soil becomes dust, washed
by flood, before care-saved seeds can grip.
She is farming our love of beef
served in sugared buns,
as she tries to raise cassava,
the *idea* of which forms,
seasoned with used to,
and our piquant insouciance.
And we still spend our time like coins
pushed through a yawn of pokies.
Even *Yes!* (beep) *You're a real winner!*
can't stir us up.

It is nibbling at us, too,
like so many fire-ants,
or a quieter plague
of dehydrated frogs.
It's bleaching a reef,
evaporating rivers into dry mouths,
with dead black gums (ah, if only puns
could save us!) and species
are taking a dive, flat-splat into the past.
Time is lapping at our door.
Listen to its parched tongue
rasping on our thin glass.

Or don't listen.
It means nothing.
That is not a clock with an old-fashioned tick.
Time means nothing, not anything at all.

The Cootamundra Wattle

Acacia baileyana

You explode in a million medals
every year –
the soft sky offset
by a universe of suns.

To see you is to smile.
The very centre of yellowness
swarming over the modest green
of your leaves.

This is the nowness of early spring.
This is the euphoric mind,
flung in joy over you,
and now flung a little too far.

Wiradjuri saw you –
first smelt you bloom
where you were set to bloom,
before another brief gold rush, and since,

but your seed spread beyond
your limits, spread like rabbits
– golden rabbits' fluffy bobtails –
from Riverina to Aotearoa

to South Africa, and you yellowed all
this land. Beauty plastered thick
becomes just a weed, and
chokes more subtle variations.

You, my lovely friend,
are the very muzak of wattle,
Vivaldi recast for electric organ
and familiar as any cat.

And just as her silky paws
hide sharpness in ubiquity,
you, named for a botanist,
bail up nature – a bushranger

gone mad, distributing gold,
slinging it from seedy bags
along the highways. No hiding.
And yet, to see you is to smile,

as you burst like yolks each year
into the quintessence of yellow.
How hard to say enough!
to the glad, luminous faces

dawning into dubious light.

A nice trip with plastics

Plastics and I have been dating.
Snakelike glad-wrapped love,
winding its way around my heart –
a wee red turtle, but shell-less, tied
in promises, mummified in hygiene.
I gag on plastics' abundance,
a seagull feeding its young pegs,
sweet pegs pretending to be sardines.
Belly full, but starving for more,
I can never get enough.
Plastics bought me a rose.
We threw away the flower
and smelt the cellophane
which bears no annoying thorn,
no unhealthy wriggle of worm.
Plastics is the love that will never die.
Never shall it decompose.

Title based on an advertisement for plastic products at Haneda airport, Japan.

Climate change (no gears)

So you spend only
a few hundred on the ancient bike
and a couple more for couriers
to bring it by road
from Victoria
in a big fart of
a delivery truck.

So you had to buy
a purple and orange
crocheted seat cover
from the United States,
which winged its way
to distant Canberra
like an ironic parrot.

And that basket!
Espied on Etsy,
woven in Thailand
(where the right reeds grow)
flown south, again,
but only seven or eight
thousand kilometres
this time.
Hardly a distance at all.

And now you ride it,
thirty minutes
every other day,
along the bike paths,
a proud little cyclist,
consumed by excellence.

Recycling a bike is good.
Cycling is good for the air.
You have done your bit.
Now breathe the breath
of safe-seated virtue.

Listen for the jangle of fallen tools.

On the death of the V8

That deep rumble, gut churning glee,
planting pure delight on tarmac
will be lost in a lighter future –
the V8 a dinosaur that farted excess
into the world's thin ring of air.
Rightly so, we say, for who needs
such a monster of pungent power?
And yet, is it wrong to grieve
for all the utes, all the Commodores
and Falcons, shined to mirror
that delicate sky, soon to zoom only
through thin streets of memory?
The skilled hands that assembled
the beasts, put the cylinders
where the cylinders needed to be,
also fading out of industrious now,
rendered redundant as corsets
or calling cards, erased from work
that made something glorious and alive,
and deadly as a steel-toothed shark.

I am no metalhead Miss Havisham,
clutching a chamois, all wept out.
And yet, when I die, I hope the chariot,
swinging down, is a lowered, purple V8.
Maybe the fetching angels
will do a few screeching blockies –
take the long way up to the clouds
where St Peter waves a chequered flag.
(The devil owns a 4-wheel drive.)

Not one cent

How much did hubby pay for that? he asks,
the Mustang, my pearl-white Pegasus,
black-striped like a two-lane freeway,
indicated with an accusatory finger.
I had driven it down the mountain,
past forest-hidden lyrebirds,
who now pluck V8 tunes in jazz solos,
shimmering. I had struggled, hard,
to keep the speed below licence-losing
on the glorious, soul-beckoning flats.
I pushed past thought, overtook it,
enjoyed the climate control.
Ah, that suburban inheritance might fund
such an inappropriate car for middle-age!
I had changed up to the devil's sweet sixth
and the metal seemed so glad to surge.
My American pony, sporting a
United Automobile Workers sticker,
symbol of the clever hands who formed it.
It should have been a Commodore,
if we still made them here, or a Falcon,
flying down the eucalyptus hills, but no,
the jobs have shifted, irrevocably gone.
And so I have found an American love.
How much did hubby pay for that?
Exactly nothing, and I tell him so.
I see him struggle to comprehend
that the striped, humming beast is mine –
my heart clutches, my brain accelerates.

Fordite

This singing ring, clasping my finger,
boasts a stone made from solid paint –
layer after layer fired into firmness
in a Ford plant in Michigan.

Opal made from the covering sprayed
on cars; hot red Mustang revving,
cooler green of some unknown auto
interspersed by a salt white river.

A little world of fordite.
And who would not say
that this ring world foretells
the baking of the bigger one

by a sun, if not hotter,
then more felt, down here below?
Perhaps we'll all have skin
melted and baked into fordite?

But right now, my Michigan agate
clasps my gear-shifter hand's
fourth finger, renders me half-car.
Android-centaur under a burning star.

Older methods of spraying cars resulted in a build-up of paint on moveable tracks, which was baked and rebaked many times. Fordite is now used as a stone in jewellery.

Spectre

Slashed into the sea,
it smiles between Gladstone
and the Cape York tip.

Whiter than a ghost's teeth,
it still grins and beckons
and whispers of what was.

Such colours grew there,
opalescent and alive,
and the flutter of fins

cruised the coral jungle;
parrots and striped teams
scrummed over living rock.

Now there are these teeth,
whitened into brilliance
by industrial stupidity.

The reef a skeleton –
or a jaw stuck forever
in a bleached rictus.

And what burnt Hamlet
to soliloquise on death
bracketing our shore?

Two thousand kilometres
grinning white forever,
and rumours of fish

corralled into memory's shoals.

Going to the coast

We drive to the coast as eager pilgrims,
seeking the stained-glass sea.
The fish beckon like misplaced angels,
promising a salty renewal.
We plunge into a baptism of waves,
a shoal of pale Canberra seals.

As if stripping off business suits,
or neat, workaday skirts
meant stripping off skin,
to find a purer self revealed.
We would surprise ourselves,
gifts unwrapped to birthday squeals.

Nonsense, of course. For there
and here are joined; work creates
this leisure lust, and the coast provides.
We speed past roos and parrots,
and topple brown mounds of wombat.
All sacrificed to questing wheels.

'The crowd was famish'd by degrees…'

From Byron's 'Darkness', 1816

George made his world too cold for life
in the volcanic year without summer.
The sun never showed itself,
modest as that widow in black,
and weird weather lashed the lake
and stranger creatures emerged;
drinking blood or created from electricity,
and the discards of the dead,
the revenant of pure science.

And now we sit in the smeltered world,
and see the crowds famish'd by degrees;
the crops of dust, the skies weeping
or obstinately dry. Look on our works,
the world must say, as some drown in
lakes of manmade excess. Ah George,
would that it were one volcano, one brief
year without a summer, as we ask
what dread creature, and know it to be us.

Lacertilian

My daughter found a common garden skink,
and it draped itself around her wrist;
a subtly jewelled bracelet, warming to energy
in the mild winter sun. Heated to sufficiency,
it flicked itself down, and ran, a quiet line,
returning to a poem of flies and grass and stones.

Nature is that which escapes mere use.
Around us, and within, it defies the neatness,
the zero sum of plans. Each pavement weed
writes itself between the flat narrative we pour,
and the mice scuttle, heroic, between combines
churning square miles of crop into white neat loaves.

And yet, the question flicks its tail inside us –
into exhausted extremity, what will not be shed?
What could remain? Nature would express itself
in rats, and some of us, and those whose exoskeleton
provides a welcome, hard umbrella. But frogs'

a cappella would no longer paint the evening
with welcome *kaplunk*. No dunnart, fat-tailed
or thin, no glory of parrot, flashing red tails
like cymbals, as they fly north and return south,
obeying an unseen, seasonal baton.
Weeds may survive storm, it's true, even storms of heat.

But when old recorded journeys, Attenboroughed,
show beauty wider and deeper than that which we
may leave; when nature plucked of emerald macaw,
bleached of coral, and whaleless by degrees arrives,
then ah! whose children will not scorn those
who planted so much less, than when skinks ran,

gleaming streams in each garden's finite space?

Feral

Feral is the weed that walks, hops or swims
that we seeded here first of all.
Like weapons in Afghanistan to fight the Russians,
they shoot back against the giver, given time.
The irony in the soil, the punchline
that keeps moving.
They are the spoonful of toad that never
helped the sugar.

The feral is the new devil;
we burn them,
use their live bodies for cricket,
run them over.
They are our scapegoats, scapetoads, scapecarp,
whipping boys for our royal, stupid selves

Varmint, pest, pets gone wild, rejigged –
dancing to their own tune.

Cane toad speaks

They are not averse to spinning me
down to bat; a squamous writhing ball.
I have been injected with petrol
and burned like the brightest beacon,
hot tribute to their dull ignorance.
The new black witch is definitely brown;
and I die on the faggots of their guilt;
the griddles of their pride.
St Lawrence of the barbie,
St Victor crushed on the road.
Cane to their Abel, they imply,
but they are the killers of will.

Yes my kiss is poison;
the princess who seeks love
inside my gnarly skin will die.
The lizard, the dog, the frog, the ibis;
even a croc may feel a bit crook,
should he smile and munch on me.
But I did not seek this menu.
I was not a tourist, keen to see
this newer, sometimes drier land.
Boffins brought me, imported buffo,
and now because I don't bite beetle,
because I will not stay still,
I am the weed that must needs die.

Yet I see them clearly, the other animals
who were here before the sugar-whites
let them slip away. They haunt me;
visions of wallaby, of recent thylacine,
of paradise parrot, flown, or hopped,
or skulked away. Those gone, those going.

Pipistrelle hovers at the edge of vision,
about to join this world of was;
the realm of still, forever.
I travel to escape the burden of vision,
these many albatrosses round my neck
(though neck was not bequeathed to me).
Dear reader, before you kill me, as you must,
look back before you, and me,

                                          and loss.

Cane toad continues

Sydney lies before me. I hitched on truck
of crescent yellow moons. Past billows
of white, past deepest blue. Refugee,
this Flying Dutchman without a sail,
and from most clogless climes.

If you want bananas, expect toads.

You planted me into Queensland's
sweet garden of delight, and now,
I expel myself upon these smiling fruit.
It is warm and green and wet in Sydney.
Takes me back to the egg, the larger egg
of jungle way back home. Death will come,
near a Bondi bikini. Seems fitting.
                    And so I hop.

Mining time

We find it, glabrous as a pearl,
in the convenient mines of the past.
We work it out with shovel,
with energetic pick, even with forks
and fingers. Time curls, an embryo,
which we transport to the present,
wrapped in silk, or boxed in velvet.
We have squandered too much time,
and need these transported years,
brought in light backpacks forward.
If we take too much time
the walls of now will collapse,
so we must be selective.
No aeons, only decades,
the occasional century,
as if we were playing cricket,
and were useful at the crease.
Whether there is time enough
to keep things going on,
is something we shall know
only if we mine more time.
There is no convenient canary
to warn of tomorrow's loss.
We string the pearls, cross
our work-worn fingers,
and wonder if our days will dim.

The canary, the pony, and the man

It sounds like a joke's first line,
a trio who walked into a bar.
But no, these are the three who
went below, swung down from the light.

One was there to pull loads
through dark roads carved
far from the sun, far from meadow,
half horse and half mole.

The bright bird, born for the sky,
would die first if the air was turning.
Now he is mere metaphor, cliché;
canary in the coal mine has had his day.

Only the man still mines.
Each day he dives down to work,
amongst rich minerals and dust –
every day rising like Lazarus.

Fry up

'Australia's climate has warmed by just over 1°C since 1910, leading
to an increase in the frequency of extreme heat events.'
'There has been a decline of around 11 per cent in April–October
rainfall in the south-east of Australia since the late 1990s.'
'Streamflow has decreased across southern Australia.'
'Oceans around Australia have warmed by around 1°C since 1910…'
– *State of the Climate 2018*, CSIRO and Bureau of Meteorology

Seventy or more years of muddy dreams
are sautéed in forty-five degrees.
Now he's belly-up and floating,
the water too low to cool his bulk.

Cotton upriver diverts the water
and helps set something rotting,
as it's cooked by climatic recipe
– and so the Murray cod is lost.

Just younger than a city called Canberra,
this awesome fish, now bloating foul.
He swam around many traps and nets,
until we snagged him on hooked ignorance

and flipped him over –
a gambler's desperate card.
Meanwhile the Irukandji, out to sea,
are floating south, and it may just be

that the smugness of those who deny
sufficient water for one living thing,
is quickly ended by a tiny other
warmly, with sharp, ironic sting.

Mo(n)de

We're snipping out that possum that lives in snow
and sewing on plucky rats like epaulettes,
their tails swishing when the wind blows.
Insects are falling like flies,
but a fringe of dead scarabs is chic,
as are legs made from a million dead frogs.
He walks the stage of the world;
is the world, to be more accurate.
We have stitched him in our own image,
demigods of tat. We talk of climate change
as if it were a fashion, hems up or down,
brown becoming the new green.
But we're all Doctor Frankenstein now,
and the world made a more murderous monster.
Chapeau! Just don't tear off your scalp,
as you remove it, to acknowledge yourself,
and your new shambles. Take a creaking bow.

My indifference is supreme, says Pluto

Educated pirates
with glasses pressed to eyes
have been concerned about me
for a century or so;
that Bostonian Lowell, with his Planet X,
as if I were a treasure chest
to be dug from the sky with intelligence
that blunt, grey, sloppy spade.
How are the canals on Mars, Percival?
(He dug them with the same dumb tool.)
They found me, and called me
after one of their puny gods,
long since passed from fashion.
They designated my moons,
Kerberos and Nix and the rest,
as if naming us made us pets.
(Though that cartoon dog
is admittedly amusing.)
And then they decided
I was not a planet at all.
Quelle horreur, I said, all fake French,
and laughed an icy laugh:
for my *froideur* occasionally cracks.
Even nitrogen has its humours.
Soon, I was a planet again,
and I hear that they intend
to send a probe to test me.
Perhaps I may take her;
a newer Persephone
to give their old tales
a frisson of authenticity.

Yet elliptical wit is the best.
I'll allow them to fret;
to classify and reclassify.
Next pass around the sun
they may all be dead,
with their sky-maps and eyes and cartoons.

The real joke is that they dare
to call my progress unpredictable.

2

Furthernear

On the couch

Some words are receding, not like sea, so much
as middle-aged hair, or the male half of it.
Being *grateful*, being *happy*, is as retro
as Olivia Newton John's neon songs.
(Now your mind locks on Xanadu
like a roller-skate wedged in a tramtrack.)
And yet, if you sip whisky, a good measure,
or two of them, while streaming jazz,
and hold the peaty gold up to the light,
and see the syncopated angel
(or some of him) dancing his submarine jig,
who could not feel joy stroke, just as your hand
strokes the fat dog's head, and his tail
smiles through the air, full all of it?
You pick his crop of shedding from your knee.
Your face is stretched into something
you near forgot, and it's not alcohol working
(or at least, not a lot). You are quietly happy,
and glad as any pup, and your soul,
yes, the whole dozy mongrel thing,
sighs, barks, and pricks its faint ears up.

Night camels

I still open cigarette packs,
unadorned with black lungs,
or floppy, cancer-kissed lips.
My hands twitch like a pianist
to fondle the magic cylinders,
perform the quick, pagan magic
of pocket lighter. My mouth
recognises a scented friend,
long kissed goodbye.
Lungs are wings sailing
on a sky of smoke,
grateful for the second wind.
Thirty years later
and I am still a night smoker,
hitched to the toboggan
of glorious tobacco.
Still an addict,
inhaling nicotine dreams.

By day, we fondle phones,
tolerate their sad blue light.
Night flicks open and glows.

Four times a week

The heft of it The set of it of it The nausea of it
The number of it The form of it The core of it
The glance of it The bruise of it The push of it
The back of it The mirrors of it The wind of it
The callous of it The iron of it The rope of it
The smile of it The spotter of it The floor of it
The dumbbells of it The sweat of it The pump of it
The rip of it The pain of it The trackies of it
The failure of it The strong of it The grimace of it
The towel of it The bench of it The joy of it
The chest of it The habit of it The groan of it
The pull of it The fear of it The legs of it
The kilos of it The runners of it The reps of it
The gloves of it The ache of it The racks of it
The barbells of it The stretch of it The blood of it
The grip of it

My body's architecture

Gone are the doric legs,
the rounded moulding of the thighs,
taut as any strand cable
under which a bridge suspends itself
in grateful punctuation.

My new, old body swings,
ropes responding to torsion,
all strong promise unravelling,
not so much broken as frayed.
A few years left until plunge.

My breasts, once high as pediments,
that strange, odd-footed word,
are willing themselves down
into architraves, lowest form
of classical decoration.

Skin is no longer carrara glass,
smooth, unpocked and sleek,
throwing back what the looker would see.
I am become adobe, roughly applied.
Bones may emerge like errant straw,

poking from the speckled finish,
which is not finished at all.
Look. The mottled surface mutates,
almost seems to seethe;
daily landslide in the bousillage.

There is no blueprint,
no draft to follow, as we pile on
years like bricks; McMansions of time.
Yet tenants of quiet joy dwell
in the unplanned additions,

the sleep-outs of the stomach,
those verandas of the upper arms.
I trace the curlicues of my eyelids,
note the gingerbreading of teeth,
their ill-matched, superfluous hues.

I stride on, swishing rococo thighs.

She who they shall call uncool

She is a pomelo amongst oranges
sarsaparilla amongst the Coke,
iceberg lettuce next to Italian mix,
or a prawn cocktail. Limping entrée.

So out of time, or simply
placed to the side of time –
fading marginalia
which no one bothers to decipher.

This is no First Folio
hidden among the Mills and Boon.
This is no new Carrie, come
to disrupt the worldwide prom.

If she festooned herself
in carefully retro frocks
people would not notice
the slightest fringe of irony.

She is somehow Costco
where she would be Paris.
Always the bulky one;
poor thick-skinned pomelo.

Pity her in passing,
with the slight squint of side-eye.
Rejig her photo with the filter
of the most mildly damned.

Not sorting it out

I know what's in the plastic bag;
some medals and a stuffed toy.
The toy was mine, but my dad
took it over when I left home,
displaying it on a pegboard
with a string around its neck;
convenient, if a tad macabre.
The medals go back further,
to a war known as The War,
when he was still English,
and doing necessary things
with ships and planes and bombs.
And if they stay in the bag,
my ex-toy, his service medals,
one part of me doesn't have to,
have to say he's dead,
can pretend we'll have the chats
we never had, and know each other
better than we ever did.
They are visas to a land existing
before possibility ceased.
And so, the bag stays closed.
The medals and the toy sealed,
so that loss is transmuted
into an occasional, lively dream.
The itch of what might have been.

Grief before grief

That mind was once fleet
as a fox after chooks,
flaunting a tail of red smarts
leaving all far behind.
Now she chases her thoughts
like a drunken tortoise
around a slow track of what? which? who? and when?
Groaning with effort, as if to birth thought.
Kindling feral anger as she remembers
that she has lost…something.

Her brain is a pizza,
picked over; a meccano
of discarded crust
or a handbag, in which she rummages,
searching for lost keys;
pulling out hole after hole after hole.
Her mind is a grim fox
with one leg wedged
in a trap,
and bantams, merciless,
flapping their wings.

Seat 13B

They swirl around, the words
of a most inappropriate quotation,
black cockatoos flapping Wilde wings.
To lose one parent
may be regarded as a misfortune;
to lose both looks like carelessness.
How careless am I, then,
I wonder, returning for the second time
from Melbourne. In the seat next to me
sits Lady Bracknell, feathers cresting,
mouthing that immortal line.
She needs no seatbelt.
She, unlike most of us,
can never die; her cut-glass voice
forever forming that glorious,
now most (in)appropriate quotation.
She stares the attendant down
as he demonstrates crash etiquette.
She never stows her bag.

Lines 4 to 7 from *The Importance of Being Earnest*. Written while returning by plane from the funeral of the poet's father, who died two months after her mother.

Intersections

Between the green and the next green
his sponge casts stripes of clean on glass.
At the red, every twentieth time, the neon bucket
is filled, then he navigates back to commander lights.
It swings, heavy as a camel's hump in his right hand.

Between frequent no thanks, and angry don't touch,
a looking past prevails, as if the drivers
were statues, marking some dubious discovery,
seeing anything but the man before them.
They sit, carefully belted and airbagged,
studying an invisible map drawn in the air.
He cleans, moving across the intersection,
a chess piece on an all grey chessboard,
diagonally adept as any Queen.
Get a job!, someone suited sneers,
above a bright tie festooned with gnomes.
Not worth answering, he moves on.
He feels anxious clouds float inside each car;
the drivers' days marked by scurried runs
between the green and the green, their shuffle,
the pungent fug of deadlines and need.
He removes the screens' flocked insects and grime.
They can see where they're not going now, he thinks.
The next driver passes a coin. Avoids his eyes.

Locus

This is the place where they meet,
to swing that one, fatal punch,
or to lose the distinction
between beer-mat
and face, the word 'glass'
shattering into a jagged verb,
through a flapping cheek of pain.
A quick slurred surgery of rage,
and two lives disfigured.
Here is the place –
the green oval,
and the young player caught by a sudden blow,
the laws of the game (whichever)
rewritten in a quick, scarlet ink.
A silhouette traced outside a pub,
shows where a look could not be borne
without a blunt, irrevocable answer.
Or the ambulance guy, scraping up
human carpaccio, where a dare
to run into traffic did not go so well,
and a bridegroom married the road.
A few trenches short of a war,
a few left-rights outside of a ring,
and this suburb could be that place.
Such a tightrope between good bloke
and prisoner, such a snip of time.
Any street can be the place,
the place where death and the men will meet.

How to make depression worse in ten easy conversational gambits, with commentary from a Real Depressed Person in brackets

Come on, pull up your socks! (As if socks are well connected synapses)

We all feel down from time to time (But what if the time is ten years?)

You've got to see the glass as half full (Merlot, methadone or meths?)

There are those worse off than you (I know that. I'm depressed, not Donald Trump)

Buy yourself something nice! (They were out of nice brains at Brains 'R Us)

Why don't you take up a hobby? (Like patronising depressed people, perhaps?)

You've got to learn to laugh at yourself! (That's why I carved a smiley mouth on my wrist)

Just get out in the fresh air and enjoy yourself! (Yeah, I'll put on my magic sport socks)

Why don't you just have a good lie down? (You do make death seem strangely attractive)

Every cloud has a silver lining (Every cliché breaks an angel's harp)

Thoughts like lollies in the cinema

– Or candy, if you prefer American terms while watching
American films, which we are. Her tiny thoughts
rattle down the aisles of her head, and the seats,
the seats in there, are all *Marie Celeste* empty,
and the film is classic *Die Hard*, but the thoughts die easy,
or are always already still born, and jaundiced,
placed in wee cinematic Jaffa coffins.
Sickening cute, kitten-blog nauseous,
happy-ending suck addicted.
Hear the tiny dirge, licking the carpet?

His thoughts, on the other hand, are Fantales,
only he never gets past the picking.
The noise is unbearable, and people shift their seats,
and still he picks like a hungry yet inept crow,
with his tiny beaky fingers pick pick pick.
The chocolate melts, nay, the toffee itself
evolves into new life forms,
and still he is picking open the sweet,
unable to extract the thought itself,
because the definitional wrapping is sticky,
and finger-beak and thought-wrap become an inextricable one.

Popcorn! These ideas seem endless!
Her hands scoop popcorn, each a little
brain, exploding, manic, shovelling,
spading ideas, devouring and chewing
and grabbing until the final assaults,
when all that are left are those hard-
nuggety hard-to-get guinea-pig-poo

unbloomed corns, and depression sets
like an unhappy ending. Until, again, it's up, up
and away, into happy, crank-crazy abundance!
It's a plane, it's a bird, it's thought itself,
exploding like a kindly machine gun,
in the jam-packed theatre of her Bruce Willis head.

On average

Once a week it happens, as regular
as a Sunday roast, or a sad Monday
morning's grey work cloak.
Sparked, perhaps, by curdled butter,
or Tuesday's unironed shirt,
a small and passing flirtation
magnified to a universe, or a joke,
punched into deadly insult. Usually,
it's just one blow harder than the norm;
a tad too deft (whether it be right or left).
But some women do fly from cliffs,
and learn the inarguable truth
of four-lettered words like 'down' and 'stop'.
Wednesdays sometimes hear a gun's retort,
or Thursdays gurgle between strong hands.
Now, if fifty were to be shot at once,
words like 'massacre' might flow,
but it's just a quiet procession of Fridays,
enacted in fifty-odd closed homes.
One died, just last Saturday, here,
when a beloved team underperformed.
And all the prayers of all the Sundays
have yet to reach the needful ears.

'Over 12 months, on average, one woman is killed every week as a result of intimate partner violence.' (White Ribbon website)

Interrobang

Erected, quickly, at the side of the road,
this confusing metal entanglement
demands full attention.
Construction opened with the words
Get out of my way!
supplemented by a tang of adjective.
Then the artist smeared his medium
over the road; the broad brush
and paint become one.
A red line points back to a bike,
pushed into a sudden ambiguity.

The bike is no longer a bike,
although the idea of bike
can still be read. One wheel
is frame-attached, and the other hangs
like a halo from a tree, as if to ride up
and away from the sad tarmac,
into the cool, kind shelter of leaves.
The seat has reversed itself
like a chicken's neck wrung
by an expert's quick hand.

A bundle, flying fluorescent rags,
punctuates the other end
of the thick red line.
It is such a small mark,
a mere hedera, ivy twisted,
huddling down into the road.
It draws the display to an end;
half Christo and half half-mast flags.
Lycra waves over pebbled flesh.

The court becomes critic;
must judge the intention
behind the sudden installation.
Mere blindness, caused by the sun?
Or sinister, as shouted words might imply?
Separating exclamation and question
takes far longer than the impact itself.
The law nudges one way or the other,
in a more sinuous play of forces.
It tries to snake its head
around the alternatives,
to unseal death.

Physics demands a simpler gift of space.

Stepping over, stepping around

It sounds like a children's game
played with an energy of rope.
Stepping over, stepping around –
I saw someone playing it.
She was wearing a pink skirt
and played it at the station.
A man sprawled, pungent as durian,
at the top of the steepish steps.
Delicately, she stepped around;
a wily politician adept
at avoiding a sticky question.
Longer legs allowed the next commuter,
the one in the suit, to step over the man.
For a moment he was an equation,
the cool guy in the suit,
and the collapsed man the vinculum
dividing the rear leg from the front.
No need for our dapper stepper
to interrupt his smartphone chatter.

And some of us step over and around
by using him for clever poems.
Grounding them in a certain reality –
restrained muggers of another's pain.

Burning the donkey

We were suspicious from the start.
What decent man brings a wife
pregnant as a pudding
into a new country, unless
he wants the child to be
a kind of hidden penny,
a nice little earner?

She was obviously mad,
whispering something about
a visitation, from behind
an annoying, coy blue veil.
We weren't sure if she meant
secret police (who are unbelievably
common, in the places these people
supposedly come from,
breeding like cane toads
in their vivid crops of lies).
She mentioned flashes and wings.
As I said, a few bats short of an attic.

He even admitted that he wasn't sure
if the kid was his, or at least
that's what we think he said.
It was hard to source a proper interpreter,
if, indeed, the language was real,
rather than a melange of all things foreign,
stirred like another pudding,
to be tongued off a soon-to-be silver spoon.
Mike said he thought Aramaic
was a perfume for men,

and we all had a good laugh,
but there was absolutely no whiff of that,
I can assure you.

It turned out to be a boy,
born in necessary seclusion,
though Mike said all the lights
turned themselves on
the moment the kid drew breath.
That was undeniably weird,
and a further example
of their lack of thanks
expressed in clever sabotage.
Lawyers even brought in presents,
breaching clear regulations.

Their poor excuse for a boat,
which had evaded all detection
and wound its feral ways to Darwin
despite navy, barnacles, tides and policy,
overladen with stink and sick and
God knows what else,
was towed back out and burnt.

All in all it was nothing remarkable,
although my skin is itching,
itching like an alien.
A nice little souvenir, no doubt about it.

The press should really leave it alone,
and focus on some bigger issues –
a Test begins tomorrow.

Three aspects of Australian racism

1.

It involves hoods,
but less KKK than DDD –
Don Dale Detention
where the kids
wear the hoods
in a stunning display
of regressive taxation.

2.

Outsourcing pain
to poorer places
which we pay
to exercise contempt
on our behalf –
washing red hands
in the convenient sea.
Who needs a wall?

3.

Protecting Islamic women
by shouting at them
on streets for wearing
religious freedom.
They wouldn't know equality
of it was unloaded at them
like a brick from a ute.
Take off that headdress.
(This is a hood.)

Seven ways to look at a sculpture

Firstly, it seemed a frozen poem,
which I read in different drafts
as I skirted around it.

Then it was time captured,
as if to trap the watchers,
and so release us from fervent rush.

By Wednesday I saw it more
as a mere mirror to catch
any cracked thought I threw at it –

but the next day it restated
its being as a question, set to
disrupt our certainties with *what*?

Friday, it seemed to push up the sky,
a small, persistent fist clenched
against wind and mess and change –

but this changed on Saturday.
The grass seemed to give birth to it
as tulip, rocket and shining tree,

which unfurled into beauty
on the stretching, languid, seventh day,
an exclamation, an endless ah!

Three ways to look at crochet

1. Cosy

Retro as a pen,
and just as useful,
this teapot sock,
this tealeaf beanie
cupping warmth in purple yarn.
I work quiet words to hold it.

2. Beaky

That insatiable hooked bill
pecking wool, ecstatic
as seagulls freestyling chips.
Her face rests blank as sand.

3. Spacey

The delicate shawl is mostly space,
nervous clicking energy forming
our possibly patternless universe.
We focus on the seeable strings, erase
the dark bits between the visible.
But without blanks between lace,
the lace itself is dumb; collapses.
(So it may be a matter of faith and grace.)

The ineffable boredom of Polonius

Hamlet had a go; stabbing him behind the arras,
which does not mean what you may think it means
if you didn't *do* Shakespeare in your degree.
But he never dies, this Polonius. He pops up as
Scoutmaster, Deputy Principal, minor MP, Mayor,
spouting cliché through his immortal mouth;

To your own self be true

he tells graduating students, some of whom
have read of him being stabbed behind the arras
and have suffered quite enough already thank you.

Youth are the future of Australia, he adds,

and I'm sure there are American and Indian and
Kyrgyzstani Poloniuses, for he has bred, you know,
splitting in two in each grave; coming up each morn
at fifty-five years.

They go on cruises, Polonii,
and spend their ineffable boredom in other places
dripping like middle-aged piss for

Travel broadens the mind

which, in this case, it clearly doesn't.

Never put off until tomorrow, he exhorts.

I feel that there must be a way to kill off his breed.
And I will work and work to find a way to eliminate
every smear of Polonius from discourse public or private.

Make hay while the sun shines,

and I am forming daggers from papier-mâché
made from the most tedious editorials still written,

in real print newspapers

crapping on about the

sacrifice of previous generations

and the inevitable

need for fiscal constraint

and I will sneak up on him, like Hamlet, but less hosey,
and force a cliché dagger down his moth-eaten throat,
though I fear he will just regurgitate the dagger,

waste not want not

he will say or

Violence is the last resort of the unintelligent and never a solution

and it is, Polonius, *oh yes it is*,
and may you choke on your sayings
and die, smearing the arras, wall, or whatever,
in horrible, tedious wisdom, like the worlds greyest
graffiti, little vombits of *save* and *safe* and *think* and

look before you leap

and it will be too late, and nobody, no nobody will weep
for the death of the boring uncle, with his inexplicable fetish
for hiding behind arrases, which is the only interesting thing
that the mouldy old sententious prick ever did.

And may flights of silverfish sing him to his rest.

A brief history of fun

First was the badly hummed tune,
or the ox bones tossed in the air in a clanking geyser,
falling down on another's serious-minded head.
Were they always solemn, those long gone ones,
when they drew fat bulls and oryx, these red hands,
on the galleried rocks? Perhaps there were giggles,
or even rude graffiti, now lost in thick patronising awe,
we spread in a blanket over far-off gusts of fun?
Stories started early, early as words, and plays
are just a quick enter stage left from camp-fire's glow.
Religious highness begets raucous jokes, for few
can live as seers, or pure priests, or silent nuns –
pilgrimages attract clowns, punch-lines, Judy
and her Punch. And speaking of funny violence,
boxers, and wrestlers and the strongmen flexed
at fairs, took on all comers, these two thousand years
or more. Roll up and see your neighbour rolled
like a cigar into a tight, burning cylinder of pain!
Clara, the pig-woman, has seen it all before, sitting
on her pink-snouted throne. As has the bearded lady;
combing out expectations from all gendered knots,
while ten coiffed poodles prance round and round and round.
Now the modern child sits and plays *3D Super Mario,*
but those fat quick Italians are heirs to Boccaccio,
though bawds may be ambushed by good Nanny Bytes.
Nothing fun is ever truly lost, whether jokes, balls, tricks, games;
they are recycled into more, later mirth.
Feasts will still be feasts, and slips always slipped,
and music and slapstick, sport and children never die.

'For services to charity…'

Her pet has such perfect teeth,
almost a Hollywood grin.
His fur is fluffy; near poodle soft,
but patting is not advisable.
Neither science nor faith
has described the neon pinkness
of the ticks that attach themselves,
attach themselves like nails
through the palms of those who caress
the pampered, fleecy mascot.
She flaunts him like stigmata;
his pedigree is unparalleled
if somewhat indeterminate.
I like to do my bit, she says,
but I couldn't do it without him,
and she plumps him up like a cloud,
a cushion fit for the better class of angel.
(Her hands alone seem immune,
quite immune to the fervent ticks.)
Yes, we have to do what we can,
she adds, her hair almost as well
coiffed as the one who hogs her lap.
Those less fortunate than I.
Those who have missed out.
Those without hope or friends.
She sighs a decorous wind.

She sets her sights on such
in the abstract. But the real one
who crossed her threshold, with
such bad teeth, and unlaced shoes
was set upon by a something,
as he rifled the drawers.

She sat, brow slightly wrinkled,
seismic fault lines replicating thought,
spraying laval concern at the police,
who tried to parse the scene.
Kindness sat on her lap and mewled.
The rings of her fingers,
set with rubies (I think)
gently tickled his locks.
(The coroner could not identify
the exact cause of death,
despite an exhaustive enquiry.)
He had been killed by something,
the thief with an unfortunate habit,
the methadone teeth and the crap tattoos.

She had to leave exactly at eight;
her camel had a needle to thread,
and she had a ball to embroider.

The precious one, the dear thing;
well, he had a maid for the evening.

Heft and leaf

Every afternoon, at three,
she takes it, sure as toast;
steeped for just four minutes,
the pot stamped with wattle,
the special rest for the strainer
the spoon laid on the saucer,
tucked under the cup's edge
like a baby, loosely swaddled.

There had been one of those,
just once, for a month, long gone,
but now she sees her in the steam,
or reflected in her own reflection
when the quiet spoon is lifted
from swirling a single lump
in the kindness of the tea,
the vision dissolving in years.

Until the next afternoon, at three.
Those who speak of mere ritual
as weakness, egregious,
never tasted the loss, knew
the milk that flowed a week after
the baby was wrapped one last time,
lowered into a muddy cradle
and covered in a rug of soil.

She taps the spoon upon the cup,
remembers a hand its size
that curled in hers, and then went
to wherever such beauty goes.
Until she knows that hand again
she gathers cup and pot and spoon.
Only so many more three o'clocks.
Only so many afternoons.

The hole

The hole in the corner scratches small holes with six legs
The hole rises from the corner and leans on my legs
The hole senses that I am crying and licks my hand
The hole takes advantage of my distraction and steals a sandwich
The hole eats its toothsome booty faster than a crocodile
The hole looks dismayed at the unwarranted criticism
The hole decides that I need a game and grabs its plastic duck
The hole minces around the lounge room with a duck shaped green tongue
The hole evades my stretched hand and takes its duck to the corner
The hole settles down on its mat with the duck near its yawning mouth
The hole fades into its holeness, and my hands stroke memory
The hole contains all sleekness and fatness and manic energy in the world
The hole in the backyard holds the bones of the one who has become the hole
The hole responds to its name, one further time, and a muted tail sweeps the air.

Who is this woman?

Who is this woman, hand outstretched,
now waving, and walking on?
I remember such a hand,
tucked in mine on endless, short walks
to school. A hand removed to scoop ice,
or to stroke a tortoiseshell cat called Sally.

Who is this woman, hair unruly,
unruly as a cat's will, such as that of Sally,
who she stroked, and taught me
that not all cats will scratch and bite,
(or not every time that you bend down)
and that pavement ice is miraculous,
in its own, slipshod manner?

This woman has seen me shrink
from a goodly part of her world,
the mothership to which she was linked
by hand, by conversation, by jokes,
words alien to other minds,
but held by our tongues in quiet glee,
to a slighter figure, surrounded by her childhood,
a hula hoop of memory.

Who is this brave woman, walking off,
walking on to Wollongong,
leaving this hand, and the paths that sported
a glorious, purring crop of cat?
My palm still glows with the bright touch,
my legs remember small steps necessitated
by shorter legs than those this woman
exercises, as she walks away.

When I go to God, I like to think
that God will look like this woman,
and how that woman was back when,
and my hand will glow, as it did,
when she held it, years ago.
I will hold a hand of light,
purring like that cat called Sally,
and walk a short miraculous path
to find myself, and wait for her.

A hard poem to market

This poem does not have a spacious deck for entertaining
after a hard day's reading itself.
It lacks a million dollar view of surrounding majestic
mountains, or even filtered sea glimpses.
A poem like this boasts no walk-in wardrobes, parents'
retreats, media rooms, or en suites.
European appliances do not grace the non-existent kitchen in
this poorly equipped poem.
Similarly, the bench tops are neither marble, stainless steel,
stone-rich, or, indeed, extant.
This poem's location is not convenient, as there are few shops,
schools, or parks nearby.
Public transport does not run within a stone's throw of this
poem's old, invisible front door.
Although this poem contains three words with the letter 'x' in
them, it lacks a so-called X Factor.
Speaking of letters, its letterbox is shaped like a snail. That is
both a lie, and a poor joke.
The poem's garden lacks any sign of birds, toads, water
features, trees, grass or space.
The curtains that cover the windows of this poem are all
wonky, smoke-coloured Venetians.
A real estate agent has hanged himself using the cords of one
of the poem's most ugly blinds.
One window has a yellowed sheet of newspaper crumpled
and pushed into a large hole.
That improvised plug is made from a page of the real estate
section of last week's local newspaper.
Out of curiosity, you remove the paper, and smooth it out, to
see if it reports something interesting.

That is because you do not know, until smoothing it, that it is from the real estate section.

It will not be interesting, but will contain far too many details about a hard poem to market.

Your hopes of finding a bargain are flattened. You leave by that bland, elusive front door.

100 or more holes in my bucket

I will never:

1. Bungee, shouting yolo
2. Use the acronym yolo, except in this poem
3. Scuba at sea (it feels like choking even in the swimming pool)
4. Have a dress made in Paris
5. Be thin enough to have a dress made in Paris
6. Be rich enough to have…well, you know by now
7. Crunch ortolan with teeth of prey
8. Tango in Buenos Aires wearing orange tango shoes
9. Tango
10. Waltz like that sweeping scene in *War and Peace* that prefigured the last glorious flyover (in the film)
11. Forget that I visited Tolstoy's estate and donned slippers fluffy as guinea pigs to shine the wooden floors
12. Waltz like Cinderella dropping a shoe like a solitary glassy dandruff
13. Open for Australia in cricket
14. Play for Australia in any sport whatsoever (though croquet is not yet kicked into touch)
15. (Censored)
16. Fly in a fighter plane
17. Set foot on the moon
18. Set anything on Mars
19. Escape the surly bonds of earth, or the merry ones, for that matter
10. Skydive screaming yolo (see bungee above)
11. Appear on the cover of any magazine, with the possible exception of *Poets 'R Us*
12. Have another child
13. Be a defender put on Buddy Franklin
14. Be an attacker trying to evade Cyril Rioli
15. Play AFL at all

16. (Censored)
17. Climb a mountain higher than Mount Kosciusko (Mount in Australia means hill elsewhere)
18. Own a gun
19. Shoot a gun
20. Hold a gun
21. Wear sunglasses like Tom Cruise in *Top Gun*
22. Jump (I can't let both feet leave the ground at once which arguably ties in with my inability to mark Buddy Franklin)
23. Start a blog comment or a post with 'Speaking as a Mum'
24. Play a musical instrument competently
25. Enjoy a ten-volume fantasy series
26. Write a ten-volume fantasy series
27. Reread *À la recherche du temps perdus* (I perdued enough temps doing it once)
28. Mistake Jonathon Franzen for Tolstoy
29. Mistake Richard Dawkins for Reason
30. Confuse faith with certainty
31. Eat dog
32. Eat cat
33. Eat durian (brain set in Anglo too early)
34. Forget what it is to be depressed
35. Suicide (that is a prayer)
36. Give up alcohol
37. Understand fatalism like a Russian
38. Write a poem about feelings which includes the word 'weep'
39. Attach a sticker to my car that says, 'I grew here. You flew here'
40. Whinge about school fees (although you should see the last bill)
41. Forget what it is to miscarry.

42. Forget what it is not to miscarry.
43. Write a book called *Carrie* (I think it's been done)
44. Judge a book by its genre
45. Sell the film rights to anything I write
46. (Censored)
47. Forget how luck has lifted me like a player to a mark (compare and contrast with 22)
48. Remember my anniversary easily
49. Regret the final time I menstruate
50. Forgive those who (censored)
51. Write a really long poem (longer than this one)
52. Lift as much as the young men in the gym, even those with execrable form
53. Become obese again (also a prayer)
54. Drive a fast lap at Mount Panorama in Holden or Ford (or even Peugeot)
55. Think that owning a European car is a sign of sophistication
56. Give up wanting a Citroën DS
57. Engage in lively debate about computer software
58. Lose my interest in sex
59. (Censored) (Sorry, that was as predictable as the shearing of narrative sheep)
60. Vote National
61. Start a sentence with 'I'm not a racist, but…'
62. Ignore cruelty
63. Be brave
64. See a cockatoo without smiling like a crest
65. Surf
66. Learn to listen without nodding or frowning or making little noises (I can be annoying)

67. Remember names
68. Speak fluent French
69. Read *À la recherche du temps perdu* in French (It keeps rearing up though and recapturing me)
70. Read Tolstoy in Russian
71. Forget the liberation of escaping school and starting university
72. Use the word 'undergraduate' as an insult
73. Listen to music as avidly as when I huddled under my blankets with a transistor
74. Tell young people that they don't know how lucky they are
75. Direct a film
76. Star in a film
77. Watch an entire Academy Awards ceremony
78. Try cocaine
79. Recite Monty Python at parties
80. Memorise all the characters in *Game of Thrones*
81. Throw myself into any social situation without a little bit of me sitting on my shoulder, half parrot and half albatross, warning and criticising
82. Write a perfect sonnet (limerick is quite likely)
83. Become a mindless gatekeeper at the Estate of Poesie (aka Downheel Abbey)
84. Write a poem without a single hint of pun
85. Cook a really good meal
86. Sell as many copies of a book as the worst selling cookbook in the land, the land being Kyrgyzstan
87. Visit Kyrgyzstan, though I have been to Uzbekistan (boasty boasty cheese on toasty)
88. Eat bacon
88. Have maple syrup on that bacon

89. Write a cookbook called *Pigging Out* or *Snout and Proud*
90. Become a knitter
91. Wear a homemade beanie in the photo on the front of my bacon cookbook
92. Forget the taste of sausages unpolluted by tofu
93. Finish this poem before lunch
94. Include the word 'weep' in this poem
95. Include a recipe in this poem, except in as much as it is a recipe
96. Pass this recipe on as an heirloom
97. Worry too much about my appropriateness or market or sales
98. Lose my love of words (another prayer)
99. (Censored)
100. End this poem with a wise saw or a blunt one

So, to sum up:

Yolo. Yolo. Yolo.

                (B

           u

                 n

          g

                   e

                   e

                        !)

www.ingramcontent.com/pod-product-compliance
Lightning Source LLC
Chambersburg PA
CBHW062146100526
44589CB00014B/1695